HAZARD, HOME

Caitlin Press Inc.
3375 Ponderosa Way
Qualicum Beach, BC V9K 2J8
www.caitlinpress.com

Text and cover design by Vici Johnstone
Cover image Anna's Hummingbird (Sah Sen)
and illustrations on pages: 3, 9, 19, 25, 39, 57, 77
courtesy Beth Wilks, creaturestudies.ca

Printed in Canada

Caitlin Press Inc. acknowledges financial support from the Government of Canada and the Canada Council for the Arts, and the Province of British Columbia through the British Columbia Arts Council and the Book Publisher's Tax Credit.

Library and Archives Canada Cataloguing in Publication

Hazard, home / Christine Lowther.
Lowther, Christine, 1967- author.
Poems.
Canadiana 20230522734 | ISBN 9781773861241 (softcover)
LCC PS8573.O898 H39 2024 | DDC C811/.54—dc23

Hazard, Home

Christine Lowther

CAITLIN PRESS 2024

Kleco, kleco to the ƛaʔuukwiiʔatḥ (Tlaoquiaht) peoples in whose territories I have composed these poems and lived so gratefully these three decades.

For those land holding, life giving miracles, the trees.

CONTENTS

SUČAS—LAND HOLDERS (TREES)

PEOPLE

WATERS

Floating on the Surface

wings of insects: termite, ant, cranefly, dragonfly

a single crabapple leaf

tide-riding expanses of pollen

tiny white petals of shore yarrow

filament of witch's hair lichen

sunlit spotted sandpiper's feather

expired minnow, belly-up

clump of moss: from a murrelet's nest?

whole white salal flowers, round as styrofoam beads

holdfast of bull kelp trailing eelgrass blade
with pipefish hitch-hiker

bleached rib of driftwood

jaw of chum salmon

knotted skull of cedar burl.

Not the Lake

When the creek's *garbledebrook* runs clear, a listener might learn where under the sod the sodding spring springs from. Everybody assumes this is the lake's creek, it emerges from the *lake*—where else? It snakes under the bog, carves through the used-to-be-lush forest, almost suffocates in skunk cabbage quagmires before spilling over boulders, onto limpeted & barnacled shore rocks. There it heightens the cove's complexity, chills & refreshes turgid tides, provides a soundtrack for dipper & resident human. The creek blows bubbles that burst as Nootka roses. The merganser sips sweet estuarine water, tips back her crested head, makes her neck long for the quenching.

The cradled course fills up with rain & discourses more loudly. With winter's roar visitors think they hear a waterfall. Nothing so pompous. The creek doesn't lecture. In summer it withdraws from the conversation, whispers only to self & salamander. But doesn't come from the lake, is not its *offspring*: that's another stream that spits out into another bay, where no person currently lives.

I have to assume this water comes—searched for throughout this dry galaxy—from a hole in the ground. All right, *dilates from Earth's deep diaphragm.* But how deep, & how far into the forest? & why? Weeks spent bushwhacking, head low, the fevered search for source. *Why do you care so much,* someone wants to know. *You already know where it ends up. I've been washing in it,* I respond. I've soaked in its sun-heated drench. Kept my garden alive with it. *I've been drinking this water unfiltered for twenty-five years,* I exclaim.

When I was young, I sang back to it.

Dear Ocean

You used to mean food, a kayak,
harbour seals, smooth surfacing porpoises,

you used to mean beauty and risk. Now you mean home:
a floating shack held in place by polypropylene lassos,

styrofoam billets, barge-hull, cookstove-anchor and cleats.
I paddle your surface in an unpoetic craft, dented and scratched

plastic. Search for striped sun stars, Turkish towel,
devil's apron, *Laminaria*. In your intertidal zone

you coax language from me even when I'm mute as a mussel.
I am a line stretched taut; the words tug.

In my frayed lifejacket, snorkel and mask
I steal up to your cloud-sized spiral of herring,

coast gilled, finned wisdom. Flashes and sparks
dance luminescent in you on rare nights.

My house ropes slacken between chop, ripple, stillness
to a seal's gentle breathing in the dark.

In the morning the fish fly
slapping the water and me awake.

What does it mean to be awakened
by a thousand leaping fish?

It's a Party

Under shimmering wings
bees cling to anise hyssop towers,
splay communally on meshes of white alyssum,
dangle from blue borage,
light up lavender, surf bee balm
and dance oregano.
Late summer they spend cooling nights
crowded to a sunflower. The rain comes.

With it, the wind. The cabin is old
and leaks. Water streams down
my bedroom window frame.
For a week it doesn't dry,
becomes a worrying stain
while the bees in the hive
in the roof above my head
fuss and buzz and build.

Turns out the streamlet is resinous to touch
and yes! sweet on the tongue.

Let them stay. Let everyone come!
Widen cracks for the bats; broaden
the barn swallows' ledge over the deck.
Boost dock flotation for that grumpy heron.
They all, all can stay.
My house oozes sticky-sweet, free honey!
I am their guest.
They were never going anywhere.

Rain Water

After days of rain the forest declaims
  in fresh streams pouring out over shore rocks,
    their adaptable acorn barnacles.
While other places, whole countries, crack and crumble,
  somehow, here, an overabundance
in new maps of timbered tributaries
  falling, flowing, flooding to the sea.
The air filled with soothing sound,
  the tide and miraculous mergansers supplied
      with fresh water.
          Rain water.
It rests atop the saline
  so they can bathe their beautiful feathers.
A system designed for them, for their benefit,
  and for a planet, and for a planet's benefit.
A wren perched on swaying salal
  sings its discovery of new water.
      Rain water. Tasting
         like the scent of trees.

Heads Up

Hail, clouds! Full of soak.
Making sun dogs, sunbows,
haloes in the cirrostratus,
rain-tailed virga, trailing jellyfish,
Van Gogh skies in daylight.
Bright fogbow reflects in still water
the eye of the mountain.
O clouds, cut the glare
with your cap and banner
astride the peak.
You carry the mist
that allows life on your planet.
We run to you for shade.
Hail, hailfall! Clouds,
let us salute you, our saviours,
our very makers.

Privilege

From pre-contact until smallpox
this place was crowded
with creek guardians,
clam diggers,
forest custodians.

Today, a floating shack
hosts the solitary descendant
of settler-immigrants
paddling a blue kayak,
clicking her phone at stratocumulus.

I empty my clouds.
She immerses herself in cool ocean
up to her chin in unshared beauty
as my tilting torrents fall
on her eyes and ears.
Does she know of the canoes?
The clippers that came after
with their flags and cannons?

She'll brag about it, maybe.
How it's only the fourth time
she's ever swum in rain,
how the high tide was so swollen
she could have glided into the forest,
petrichor floating everywhere,
strange sight of her limbs
in russet hued water,
the impression of trees marching
into the sea. Or falling.
The blur where creek water slides
in among the salt.
How she side-stroked
pelted by my kisses
of rain on her hair
rain on her tear ducts
rain on her laughing lips.

At Mosquito Creek

It's noisy. Beyond the frozen dam, unreachable, a tall bank green with crane's-bill and bryum moss. A creekbed berm that holds huge, stiff hanging deer ferns and hundreds of long icicles. Before the creek itself, whole slopes of rippled ice. Enough strength to contain sunlight, encase sword ferns and liverworts in stasis. Blebs of air, too. Are there animals in there who will live again? We break off silver spears and suck them, our gaze fixed on foliage now locked as ice-dreadlocks poised over white rapids. No safe way to reach the waterfall.

Perhaps Healed

To listen for summer is like listening for a poem.
Through the fog a chittering of raccoons
in the littoral zone,
their careful percussion of stone-turning
in search of crabs, isopods, chitons.
Such is the compulsion toward defining a season.
The seal, resting below deck, groans.
This coast is baffled
—a cold hand held over the harbour's mouth,
opal glaze muffling the setting sun.
Columns of mist
mimic the forest's front row
of hemlock and cedar,
that same grace in form and movement,
ritual moving over water,
a ceremony without invitation, silent.
The sun sets and night's ink
blends slowly from treeline into sky,
silhouettes' outlines dissolving
as if by their own distinguished design.
Along this precise timeline
leaf-rustle by molecule
the world stills into deepening quiet
like a gradual falling-to-sleep,
the faces of my loneliness retreating.
How right: a day expunged by vapour,
events softened, numbed, perhaps healed
with the rising of some sweet scent.
Young people's voices carry over water, strum
of acoustic guitar from a neighbouring floathouse.
The stars are sealed off, there is no hope
of northern lights, of meteor showers.
The damp cave of night is held close, closed.

SOUNDS

Hummadruz

What is this hum, and will it become a growl, then a roar?
This is miles from town. Boats are scarce.
High jets burn white paths across the sunlit sky,
but they pass and are gone. Sounds are
robins singing, tides flooding and receding,
currents swirling and sliding,
wind suthering in alder leaves
and spruce boughs, sifting through pine:
both needle and cone.
Sounds are *quick*-three-*beers!* calls of
olive-sided flycatchers,
echoing drills of pileated woodpeckers,
the swelling creek receiving rain.
Miles from town, no mining or logging.
Miles from town, no airstrip or generator.
Only at night, sometimes, the hum.
Northwest, Catface as the crow flies:
just a few cabins there. Miles away, over water
and wooded land. Can they hear it too?
When darkness should bring silence,
stars glimmer mutely—what is this hum,
and will it become a growl, then a roar?

Hummadruz is "a noise in the air that you can't identify, or a sound in the landscape whose source is unlocatable." *Landmarks*, p. 190, Robert Macfarlane quoting Richard Skelton in conversation. *Suthering* is the "noise of the wind through the trees (John Clare) poetic," *Landmarks*, p. 310.

HAZARD, HOME

Listen From

Not knowing is a state of being to work with.

The town dock rings with wedding cheers, boozy hollering,
tied boats rocking in wind or wake. Lifesuits swish on sight seers
marching down the ramp. Floatplanes untie, taxi into the harbour
and take off. Blast the evening air.

But early morning, while the revellers sleep,
a multitude of small splashes
like haphazard rain:
the fish are many and hungry.
It's low tide and raccoons chitter
between grounded boats.
Under the walkway the masked animals
find food in the mud.

Loud breaths and snorts from dark water farther out:
river otter, sea otter, harbour seal or sea lion?
One individual, or more?
Not knowing is a state of being to listen from.
Pre-dawn *keer* cries of murrelets
cue the day's beginning.
Kingfishers ratchet raucously, suddenly,
with or without fish in their bills.

At first human footfall on the ramp, a great blue heron lifts off the dock.
Flaps cupped grey wings and screams its harsh *kraaak* to wake the dead,
or at least the hungover. Soon guide boats will be warming up twin motors,
altering the soundscape again. I want to hear what I can't identify.

The Listening Dark

Quit writing nature poems, he said.
Stop writing tragic-childhood poems, she said.
In the dark night, the barn-arch
of the cabin roof, hump of hill,
curve of cove, jumble of shoreline,
relief of headland shaggy with trees,
distant triple rise of mountain
—all were black and still
as if listening.
The water's pinpricks of light,
a million mouths opening and closing.
  Pilchards! a common fish,
  they swim like fast torches.
  They swim under falling stars.
  They swim under aurorae.
  A whole world's prey, they endure,
  spiral in their timeless circuits
  around the bay, their turns of fin and scale
  shooting stars in the water.
The first eight years of anyone's life
shaped us forever or,
after much work, left a residue
of triggers in the flame of day.
Night is counter-argument, with shivers of surprise:
a flycatcher's fast whistle,
a small owl's hoots,
the living, listening water,
a balm of breeze
that lifts the unbearable heat.

Identify

Let's invest in quieter devices
hear the otter family coming
the adults' whistles and low pulsing chuckles
the young one's chirp.

From the forest comes the sound
of a grouse drumming to attract a mate.
We'll try to record it
but the creek will drown us out.
Both cadences contain puzzles,
emerge from the forest
change with the seasons.

House guests point out
that they listen differently here,
most sounds not human-made.
Together we'll make a game of trying
to identify rustles and squeaks
without aid of any app.

Calls and songs of known birds
side by side with those unknown:
there is yet so much to learn.

Bees' buzzing ceases in sudden silence:
they doze, defying gravity
on salal's hanging stamens.

Flutterings and scurryings in the underbrush:
we are not alone. Full branches cracking, the huffing breaths
of a black bear: it has caught our scent.

A soft-voiced side-stream waits for generous clouds;
a chattering course is replenished.
A jay's rasp-call opens the air
between eternal creek and sharp beak.
Ah! to know that blue black shadow's comic, cosmic voice.

Keen

A snapping twig announces the mother's presence.
Her progress parts branches, she trots out onto
the shore grass and sea asparagus,
in her mouth a black wing
on its hinge of red gore.
Her fur ripples in patches of grey, black and ginger.
There is a perk in her step—
she is travelling back to her pups, successful.
She crosses the creek, enters the forest.
I can no longer see her, and I scour
every bird guide to know whose wing
she carried. Sooty grouse or raven
but I'll never know, not really.
That night the whole pack troops back
over the rocks, pups whisper-whining
in the near-dark, their first time
back across the creek
and over softer land, so much of it.
Long, long may it be so!
From a distance, the howling rises:
the pups yipping and yelping their keen
instincts and heritage, voices of family,
song of survival,
for the moment
sated and unafraid.

BIRDS

Mergansers

Mother is a raft, ridden
by six soft ducklings
three more trailing close behind
under round brown helmets of down,
spotty as fawns.
On shore they crowd up to her:
Mother is a roof to cram under,
shelter from the rain.
Fishing in the shallows
she quacks with alarm, guttural escalation
and they charge after her;
where the dreaded mink?
But it's a loon, another poem rider,
black and white and low in the water.
It can't follow so close to the rocks.

Oh Merganser, Merganser!
Put one in every stanzer.
Nine namedrops for the scooting ducklings
catching their own fish,
many more for Mother
defending them with her life.
Fluffy cuddlies! To them she is
a shield of feathers
a winged boat
a shelter of heat and bones
spike-crested Mama
who hatched them in an ancient tree
and dared them to jump.

Pop-up Grebe

Closer and closer you appear
little grebe,
popping up between waves.
Float there while hummingbirds
criss-cross above your head, unnoticed.
They are more substantial.
Gaunt grebe,
the loon is thrice your size.
Tiny moulting grebe, did someone
splotch ink marks over your neck
then wipe their hands
on your juvenal wings?
Oh grey mess, titchy grebe,
are you just young
or still in winter plumage?
Horned grebe or vagrant Eared,
you don't match the guidebook.
Smidgen-specimen. Sooty.
You catch and eat a minnow
smaller than my pinky.
But sudden vast absence!
You blink out behind a wave.
The water claims you again.

Pecking Order

The rufous' relentless refusal to share, then
the male's shuttling tail-dance in the female's face,
to hypnotize or intimidate—oscillate in air—
a buzzing yo-yo trick to woo or bully.
She keeps her perch, fans her tail feathers.

Crows gang up on a fledgling robin,
tear it to pieces. Excruciating world!
Crows, humans' favourite fetish, bully jays,
jays turn and dare red-eyed towhees,
towhees lunge at sparrows,
sparrows menace juncos,
the orange, barred varied thrush chases all away
but is the most skittish of humans.
The male junco returns, charges at his mate,
guards the scattered sunflower seeds
for himself. Some provider.

But the tiniest female junco
flits, scratches and jumps,
always on her toes,
pecks for seeds when she can,
leaps over the fat sparrow.
Darts around in her twitchy
dance for food.

Raven

Raven cannot be co-opted
by a seedy drinking joint
down at the docks.
Not by a fanged nightclub
in a TV vampire series,
nor by Stark Raven, a prisoners'
rights show on alternative radio.
Not by a person's name, given or chosen,
nor by Raven: western Canada's one-stop
source for truck accessories
since 1977. Wide load.

Air sieves through black feathers,
stroking the clouds, the sound
of fast flight.
Fighting mid-sky, claws up
to repel persistent crows,
spinning over, claws down
to plague eagles:
their young scream like vixens,
their elders call like evolution
cupped in hands of air
echoing off mountainsides.

In some places ravens are so plentiful
their voices thicken and fall,
new calls come from
the ground—stand still and feel them
speaking in your soles,
your bones and body their conduit.

When the open palm of sky
holds out a sound not recognized,
it will be Raven's call, melodious,
a voice like caves,
darktime in daylight,
reminding.

A cry that sculpts skies,
cuts through winds, carves
a whole language
from one bird's shaggy throat.

Belted Kingfishers

It was just the nephew and me; we decided to take a drift
in the kayaks with our beers, follow the shade.
Three kingfishers were making a fuss, you know how they are.
Chasing each other, staccato scolding, aerial
twists and turns, graceful surprises, clean colours.
Parents and a fledgling? *Time to branch out on your own.*
Fledglings and a parent? *Why have you stopped feeding us? Get on it!*
Mates and an interloper? *Scram! We're the jealous type!*
But no-one seemed territorial, rather testing their skills,
joyed by a birthright of open air, light feathers, strong wings.
Finally the nephew decided: three fledglings.
Through his binoculars, he saw rufous markings
only on their flanks. Shortish bills as yet.
Check this *out! Can you do that? Isn't this* wild?
Departed parents forgotten. *Look how high!*
By now they'll have learned to hover and plunge,
slap minnows against their perch,
build a burrow, raise their own young.

Marbled Murrelets

It must be truly ancient.
Tall, too, and away from edges.
We need a furrowed, flawed specimen

its wide horizontal branches
graced with cozy deformities
thickly furred, and much of the time, fogged.

Fir, spruce, hemlock or cedar
: and a different tree each year.
Our shallow nest protected by other boughs

against rain, wind and predators
must be high above the ground
and not impossibly far from the ocean.

Unless we run hard across saliferous water,
a high branch is our only way
to successful take-off. We cannot walk on land.

We forage from and roost on the sea
until I enter the forest, lay a single egg.
My chick will eat sparingly

on our commuting schedule.
My fledgling's first flight
must take it to salt water.

Dawn brings our piercing calls,
fear of corvids, urgent forest-love
and the hungry miracle that waits there.

Marbled murrelets are endangered due to loss of habitat (old growth forests).

Swainson's Thrush

In a book supposed to be about west coast life in general, the authors—and there are many—keep referring to the same bird. The memory of its rising spiral-song haunts them all winter with elbow-tugs to mystery's core. Other books, other authors, join in. They wait to hear it every spring, counting down, *any day now*. Victoria May 19, camas meadow, singing from Garry oaks. Tofino May 21, late afternoon conifer shore-forest. Four days later than last year. Every song as if testing the air, the after-silence feather-soft. A plain-Jane bird opens its bill and enters their marrow, a beauty that blindsides them awake, as if *wonder* were a new word.

"Common" Loon

I wish you could see the loon dive down;
it's the prettiest thing in the world.
The loon, and the dive itself.
The bird's ebony, steep forehead so smooth and clean,
the smart black collar under a striped torc,
the breast so spotlessly white
speeding down on a perfect diagonal
to the depths of the sea for food.
What is this stunner? A diver, a water bird
whose back is like the star-crammed night.
The loon fishes under the deck.
If you stand on the edge,
you can look straight down
upon its wings, but the water
is too dark to spy the webbed feet
set back, propelling forward.
Remember to watch for the surfacing.
For surprise on the velvet face.

Nighthawks

Nighthawks can attach themselves to you in a particular way. As birds of dawn and dusk, they come when your thoughts are already lingering on deeper topics than work or meals.
    —Briony Penn

Heard in the damnedest of places: among skyscrapers, in a teen vampire movie, over a clearcut. Their seasonal migrations last only twelve weeks. On the gulf islands they seem to thrive on storms, the *boom* of their dives more thrilling than a crack of thunder. Dusk-divers. Mouths wide as they fly, insect-seeking. Sharing with bats a stomach full of mosquitos, blackflies, winged ants and beetles. Far less common than their name. Wind swallowers. "Peent," they call, and *boom* goes the shifting of primary wing feathers shuffled by air. The opposite voices of true summer heard at last, if sought.

Nighthawks "are occasionally called 'booming swallows' in folk discourse; and their gaping, insect-seeking mouths have, in some French-Canadian regions, earned them the fanciful folk-name of engoulevent (meaning 'wind-swallower')." —Harvey Thommasen and Kevin Hutchings, *Birds of the Raincoast: Habits and Habitat.* Harbour Publishing, 2004, Madeira Park, BC.

Eagle

On the descent, you hang-glided overhead: pantaloons extended, talons poised. You careened past to speedland like a wakeboarder on the water, struck, scored the surface. Came up empty, took off to harangue the fish hawk. Stole the osprey's offspring's meal. Another day you veered away in surprise when you realized it was my head on the water (attached to my swimming, startled body). Yet another day you swiped the water for a fish—missed—swamped—had to paddle-wheel to shore with your broad, wet wings, and clamber up on the rocks with those clawed yellow feet. Today you caught an eel and flew away across the harbour with it dangling, your fellows in hot pursuit.

Nearly Grown

The juvenile mergansers are back.
I've wondered where they've been
and how many survived
since they were small enough to ride
six at a time on their mother's back.

The juveniles are on and off
the half-burnt breakwater log.
There are eleven of them still
—no sign of the mother.
Because of them I don't work in the greenhouse,
use the outhouse,
or step on my floor's creaky seams.

I tip-toe around and spy on them.
Some of them are larger than others now.
Some of them have more pronounced
head-crests than others.
Some have more wing colours.
Could this be more than one brood,
joined together for company?

Now they preen and rest on the log
or re-enter the water,
diving under their bubbles,
catching fish skillfully.
They've been doing this all day.

SUČAS—
LAND HOLDERS

(TREES)

Having read the last eleven lines of a poem about hemlocks

an odd rushing fills my ears;
the staggering science of trees
lifts hairs from my scalp.
I grab the binoculars,
get outside and leave the trail
risk thorns and ticks to approach
an ancient cedar I've admired for decades
but never bushwhacked up to.

> What are you?
> Giant wind-surfing limbs,
> cinnamon-grey bark
> ribboning over curves, burls
> where other branches used to be
> until no longer needed,
> your crown a stag's head.

Red cedars can live with a higher ratio
of decayed to living wood than anybody else.
This one's so old its trunk has divided into two
massive, splayed boles
and the mound it's on—what used to be a nurse log
a thousand years ago—is shared with a strange
slim sibling, straight and unbranched nearly all
the way up. At first I think pine
but through the binoculars
the flat, blunt needles suggest hemlock.
Its high crown drops
a single strand of spider silk
catching waves of light
reflected by breakers on the beach far below us.

Half an hour later my clothes are damp and twigged,
brown with log duff, binoculars caked,
glasses smeared, cap caught up
on salal bough, neck sore from looking up.
I've taken enough photos to satisfy obsession,
finally quit clicking at the split
between the two cedar trunks when

a female Anna's hummingbird
appears at the far end
as if vibrating.
I freeze.
She zooms through the rift
hums from knot to Dicranum tuft to salal stem
to my face. For a moment,
studies my unblinking eyes.

Hazard, Home

A red-breasted sapsucker drills a cedar's cambium
in *neat punctured rows*. Drinks when the sapwells fill and flow.
Feeds on attracted insects, and flies off.
A rufous hummingbird flashes in for its share.

Room is made for martens when time hollows a hemlock:
the arborists' hazard, home to more scufflers and singers.
It's the dying that reinvigorates; roosts, rests, hidden shelters,
clinging of bat claw under flap of loose bark.

A broken-topped safe house, pocked, naked,
a pine primed for primary cavity excavators
like that double-keystone-species sapsucker,
who gouges, inhabits, and departs.
A new home for secondary cavity nesters:
Chickadees.   Wrens.   Tree swallows.

Phrase "neat punctured rows" used with permission of the publisher, Lone Pine Publishing, from *Wildlife & Trees in British Columbia* by Fenger, Manning, Cooper, Guy and Bradford, 2006.

Alders I

My home is a shake box floating on a moat
gazing across at the shore's red alders
—short-lived catkin makers, leafed eccentrics
squeezed between shoulders of conifers
holding in the carbon that would hurt us.
I'm framed on the outside by cedar shakes,
inside by spruce guitar wall panels.
Squiggled grain of plywood floor
is like wave rivulets on sand.

Mornings I head off with my paddle
say hello to all the alders
drinking daylight
from where the tide tickles their feet.
Some are mere whips or starvelings.
Others brim leaf-whelm every spring.
Others are long lived, sport cranks,
crambles and cags but no more leaves.
Still others are what's left of brokeneck snags.
I visit 'em all, the only deciduous species here
not counting shrubs, and who would? (I would)

Whip: thin tree with a very small crown reaching into the upper canopy (forestry)
Starveling: ailing tree (forestry)
Leaf-whelmed: in such dense foliage that sight is extremely limited (poetic)
Crank: dead branch of a tree (Cotswolds)
Cramble: boughs or branches of crooked and angular growth (Yorkshire)
Cag: stump of a branch protruding from the tree (Herefordshire)
Brokeneck: tree whose main stem has been snapped by the wind (forestry)
All from *Landmarks* by Robert MacFarlane.

Alders II: Cutting

Before and after the 2015 Nanaimo Cascadia Poetry Festival

The other poets dispersed
to their particular ecosystems;
only my return, and solitude, waited.
Morning streets offered trees
in their May flush, some in bloom:
rowan and dogwood,
hawthorn and horse chestnut.
Pruned and shorn to avoid hydro lines,
their remaining branches burst luxuriant, sent
whispered blessings down on every passing head—

Cut us, we'll love you.
I stepped off the curb, followed a railway's
diagonal track to bluebells,
copious climbing ivy, arching alders
who stretched green-splashed limbs
from their grey trunks,
soft toothed leaves
not yet at full size or strength
like our poems in their early drafts
still cutting their baby teeth.

More Perilous than a Leaning Tree

What Bob McDonald means by *feedback loop*—
climate change is caused by deforestation,
deforestation is caused by climate change.

Canadian rainforests were not described at school.
We didn't learn of their existence
until years later in Pacheedaht territory
where we climbed trees, swam the river,
blocked the logging road with sticks,
boulders, fallen branches,
even dragged stumps from the clearcuts,
made log-and-hammock tripods,
padlocked ourselves,
then threw on our shovels as the crummy arrived.

We wanted to keep candelabra cedars pitchforking the sky.

Back then we wore our fleece all summer
and called the second month Fogust.
Now it's Fire, smoke and sweat
as trees fall to greed and grief
before and after the solstice storm
that hurled down hundreds more,
opening the wind-funnelled gorges
to glare and sorrow and solastalgia.

Politicians want to prevent more fires
by pulling out the understorey,
turning Turtle Island's habitats
into lungless brown-mossed parks.
Over-cautious arborists afraid of trees and lawsuits
climb into their dangerous trucks and drive.

Scrubby

Dear forest,
let's crack through concrete!
A blast for a blast!
Ƛaakašiis, carbon curer
migratory navigator
biodiversity's chaise lounge
maintainer of heartbeats
humble habitat, home
—dearest forest,
part of the greater Tribal Park
crowding the islets
bending over the surging inlets
sending your fallen splashing across
clear salmon streams…

the mayor sat on a *rhedynog* log
dozens of moss and fern species
dyrys around her feet and
called you "scrubby"
to justify her plan
for cubicles and cars
townhouses in heat domes.
Oh photosynthesis and oxygen,
she continued colonized
insult to juryless injurious
"District Lot #114."
"We put houses where there were
rocks and trees."
As if that were an achievement! Success!
Frond nation, thwack back!
Oh generous life sustainer
our breath provided by you
she would not wake to your already-shelter
your sphagnum and sundew
your snoozing snakes, scent of twinflower
just more acres to be hacked away
killed and drilled
replacing what made her town
irreplaceable.

Rhedynog: abounding with ferns (Welsh)

Dyrys: tangled, thorny, wild (Welsh)

Both from MacFarlane.

ƛaakašiis (Tlaa-kaa-shiis): the local ƛaʔuukwiiʔatḥ (Tlaoquiaht) nation's word for what was later renamed Tonquin Park by white settlers in the Tofino area.

Flash Mob: My Name is Not District Lot 114

District Planner to Municipal Council:
The subject property is currently vacant, undeveloped land.

That land, leaping up:
You make me sound like a dusty, forgotten paddock. On the contrary! I am inhabited, living land. Home to countless birds, mammals, amphibians and invertebrates who dwell nowhere else.

I was once clay, sand, rock, and roots. These were *developed* by the current bio-network: temperate-zone rainforest, a peak habitat. Globally rare!

Your plan is to re-develop, or over-develop. You will be the first to make me vacant. Strip my fruitfulness, then trammel me with vehicles and walled units on new surfaces usable only to you and your kind. Trees dismembered and removed, roots pulled up, clay compressed, rocks shattered. I cannot breathe under gravel or cement. I'll be buried alive.

Your Official Community Plan advocates for "human-oriented development." Perhaps this should be changed to Human-Oriented Growth, or HOG, as you already monopolize the narrow peninsula. What about the bears, cougars, and wolves when they wander onto your parking lot, looking for their favourite resting spot? Do you have a relocation plan in place, other than your melancholic conservation officer with his gun?

V2A, or Vision to Action, planning document:
Ecosystems are healthy and flourishing, biodiversity is preserved, and wilderness is protected. Residents and visitors enjoy clean air and water, and a dark night sky.

The land:
The largest footprint in your plan to erase and re-develop me is your tire-print. Humans treat driving as a right instead of a privilege. Diversity is suffocated by concrete. The way I am now, *forest*, sequesters carbon. Keeps you alive and well, counteracts exhaust and exhaustion. You idle, I produce clean air. See me not as empty, available. See me as your preserver, already populated; see me as your children's and grandchildren's future.

As a complex and expert symbionment of reciprocities, I am biodiverse. "Wilderness" is a more problematic term. There is no "middle of nowhere" or "wasteland." I once had respectful human caretakers who were in turn taken care of by me: their ancestral garden. We were rich and full together. Until: you. A new world view, so commanding it dims the stars.

The air:
I am not clean with running vehicles and airplanes. I am not clean with wildfire smoke and smog. Choose your summers: blue sky or red? My windstorms are so fierce.

The wetland:
I am clean as long as your cars don't leak or ooze, so long as you don't make rainbow slicks on my surface and poison the waterfowl. Fumes get in my eyes and my clouds rain acidic. Ban your styrofoam, by the way. Maintain catchment barrels to sustain yourselves; don't drain the land. Drink the sky. I'm safe with an intact forest, though none of us can escape the changes. Dance down the rain.

The night sky:
Now you see the stars, now you don't. They were, are, and will be here. I can't compete with your glaring lights, your fear of the dark. I can't compete with smoke or smog. Nor can the migrating flocks that need me, us.

Appendix 1:
Mitigation measures will be carefully followed during construction to protect the water courses.

The water courses:
Plan writers in offices are a long way from diggers and movers down here in the mud. Destruction comes before construction. The heavy boots bring the spinning tread and screaming chainsaws, clogging my cleanse, damming my direction, leaving cigarette butts and plastic bits. Where will frogs and salamanders go? They must be considered, or they will be crushed.

The frogs and salamanders:
You could slow down. We have nowhere else to go.

The songbirds, woodpeckers, kingfishers, and dippers:
We're really busy. Let's just say we've nested here for millennia.

The salal:
Why don't you like me? Look closely. Have you seen my soft, light green new leaves in springtime? Look for them alongside unfurling fiddleheads. You could stop paving now. There are other ways to move through the world, different ways to grow.

The trees:
What goes around comes around. Such deep sorrow.

The land:
You cannot protect water if you skin my surface. Could you retrain yourselves to see me as already living, occupied, prospering? My name is not DL 114. Notice how sweet the air is among the trees. You could make time for stargazing. Could remember water as connected, alive, inhabited. Your survival depends on us remaining whole. You could befriend all of us, recognize us as simultaneously fragile and strong.

Thanks to Glenn Albrecht for the term "symbionment" from his essay "Solastalgia and the New Mourning" in *Mourning Nature: Hope at the Heart of Ecological Loss & Grief* edited by Ashlee Cunsolo and Karen Landman, McGill-Queen's University Press, 2017: "[H]umans are embedded within what we might otherwise term the environment. ... I have decided that we actually *all* live in the 'symbionment.' This term has its origins in the word 'symbiosis,' which in turn is from the Greek *sumbiōsis* (companionship), *sumbioun* (to live together), and *sumbios* (living together). Within the symbionment we live together with relatively harmonious companionship or a state of ecosystem health between ourselves and other beings." p. 303.

Also thanks to Joanna Streetly for the term "bio-network."
Ⱡaʔuukwiiʔatḥ nation member Gisele Martin teaches how the rainforest was her people's ancestral garden.

Statements by District staff, V2A document and Appendix 1 are actual quotes.

To-Do List for Town Tree Protectors

Write to the local newsroom: describe how trees matter rather a lot.
Write to council with questions & friendly suggestions.
Spread far & wide the shocker that a tree has to be mature to begin
sequestering carbon, so keeping ancients is better than planting newbies.
Lobby individual councillors, known for years.
Point out how ample shade mitigates a heat dome;
a full canopy buffers a red sun & breaks up smoke.
Write to the manager of public spaces, who once saved your life.
Write to the sustainability director, who jogs your favourite beach.
Write to developers. Beg for new, climate-smart plans.
Write to the town planner: propose that trees matter rather a lot.
Relate how standing dead trees are vital to birds & wildlife,
while not automatically hazardous to humans. How, in fact, their roots
soak up rain water, prevent floods. How intact forests save lives.
Write to the public works head, who directs arborists.
Write to arborists begging them to assess trees less warily & more creatively.
Remind land owners it's ok to brace & buttress leaning or hollow trunks;
it's all right to guard their pines for the atmospheric river.
Write to the local health authority pleading for the lives of the last two trees
standing tall near the new heli-pad zone.
Count trees, stumps & rings, everywhere between Načiks and the cemetery.
Make inventory lists of significant trees, those lost, and those planted
(the shortest list of all).
Agree to research other small towns' tree protection bylaws
for the busy sustainability manager.

Write to the national park; tell them you are a cyclist.
Ask if they will budge on killing 2,000 trees for a bike path.
Write facebook posts: detail how trees matter rather a lot.
Follow advice from a councillor to re-form the old activist group
to add credibility & delegate tasks. Branch out. Proclaim the unspoken shame:
these trees are all on stolen ƛaʔuukwiiʔatḥ land.
Stay on top of emotions. Climb a trunk to cry on. Funnel despair into a raging poem
& keep your smile steady for every meeting with authorities or fallers.

Mourn the heli-pad trees; remember them—red maple, tall green oak, ancient hemlocks
preceding them. How they shaded & beautified hospital patients' rooms, sped healing.
Mourn the bike path cedars, airport alders, boles, burls, nests, smoking debris piles.
Enter fall zones & talk to the people holding chainsaws.
When they say they're calling the cops offer them your phone
because you've got the bylaw enforcement officer on the line,
& you've already called the cops. Strap on your goggles.
Keep in mind there are times to depart fall zones & times to stay.

To the Trees

More controversial than pipelines,
value-adding or blocking the view,
tolerated or bulldozed,
admired or severed at your base,
fought for or discarded,
protected or dismembered,
grieved or forgotten,
shored up with brace, buttress, and guy wires
or assessed, deemed hazardous, and doomed,
gated and guarded
or mass murdered and profited from:
Lung filler, life giver, defend yourself!
Nest host, network, sculpture, poem,
fling your killers' chainsaws from their
unworthy graspers! Suck the air
from their chests.
Desiccate their skin.
Shade them no more
and they will burn
as you adapt
to a heating world.

The Child

In the boat you looked up at the mountain and said
But the bare crowns—the trees are dead.

You might be used to tree farms, plantations:
rows of the young not allowed to live
until their crowns become noble and unclad.
Ancient forest includes all ages,
a mix of green tops and grey.

And the child dreamed
the leaning loose-branched old maple
down the end of their street
could have been allowed to live.

Docking. And you said
That towering old snag could fall at any minute.

Or in several centuries. It stands dead
almost as long as it stood alive.
An osprey's lookout perch.
A reaching reminder of how tall
the whole forest used to be.

And the child dreamed
of the snag even taller, alive and green,
bright with its bare and feathered future.

At the table you studied the forest
through the window, with binoculars.
There's another soaring old snag in there
you said. *Far in. Smooth bark
bleached white by centuries of sun.*

There's no trail to it. A scarred,
branchless grey spear prods the clouds
somewhere back there.
Once in a while it emerges into view.

And the child dreamed of pygmy-owls
living secretly inside the white snag,
and of black bears in the grey spear
suckling in a high-entry maternity den.

Leaving, you said *Some decay is good.*

And the child dreamed
of the braced trees in all the cities of Japan.
And the child arrived home
gathered neighbours, cables, tools
built support structures
to keep the trees and people safe.

"Coastal black bears in particular are highly dependent on wildlife trees for shelter from the
heavy winter rains. Dens in hollow trees may be from ground level to 15 m above the ground,
and the entry is often from the top of the tree." *Wildlife & Trees in British Columbia*, p. 255.
This poem was twigged by Pat Lowther's "Early Winters" and by a boat ride with my friend
Ross Harvey.

PEOPLE

"My" Bears

The female that time, so nonchalant, eating salal flowers
while her yearling crashed through the bush
and proudly stood, placed two front paws up
on the log beside her. She kept munching.

The mate this year, all heft and gloss,
hurrying after her, his huge feet
grasping sea lettuce-slippery rocks
no hazard to him. His still-living forebears
remember when I wasn't here yet.
They snuffled for crabs at their ease.
Grazed the shore grass without audience.

She was back last night exactly three hours
after two tongue-lolling wolves.
Alone. She could smell them.
Crunching on sea asparagus,
she headed in the opposite direction
into the forest, where night had fallen.

And the hulking bruin long ago
who sought relief from a hot afternoon.
Tags on both ears, head like a boulder,
he ignored me and a pestering raven,
and swam away southwest
in the clean cold sea
looking for a shallow, softer shore
that could take his weight.
Somewhere in the shade.

To Do in ƛaʔuukwiiʔatḥ Haʼhuulthii: the tourism brochure

Zip up some raingear and stroll the beach
to see the wind-blown stacks of rain.
Keep surfers' dogs company.
Don't let them chase birds.

Pore over miles of sand,
catch sight of *Velella velella*'s tiny blue sails.
Take note of beach hoppers and worm casings
choked with styrofoam beads. Pick up the beads
and the cigarette butts.

Trip over drift logs in dripping sea caves,
snarls of storm-tossed bull kelp.
Study tidepools for anemones, sculpins,
marooned moon jellies. Eyes only.
Keep your tide chart handy.
Plan for power outages.

This is cougar habitat. Paint eyes
on the back of your hat
and head out with a telescope.
Feel for the rare,
textured trunks of yew.

Allow yourself to be pierced
by salmonberry thorns.
Bleed onto roots, into moss.
Let this place both mesmerize
and alert you. Leave only your cells
on its bark. Bathe in the bioluminescence.

Down on the docks, ask for carvers. Commission art.
Take in the class gap, racial divisions, empty mansions,
having to choose between housing and trees,
aftershocks of attempted genocide.
Try to look through decolonized eyes.
Call Tofino Načiks or Kwisaqs.

After the remote inlet...

a docked floatplane's revving engine dooms eardrums.
Up the ramp, men in machines are remaking Main Street.
Across from the elementary school a chipper and a cherry picker
vibrate the sidewalk. Men are chainsawing to death two raccoon trees
piece by piece from top to bottom.

At the school, workers dismantle the swing-set, our inventions
smearing dirt over the ball field next to the alder trail.
I panic and call the District, but it's only a culvert going in.

All winter developers erased life,
bulldozed and blasted its roots,
bent and bruised the air, lacerated hearts.
Now summer weed whackers shake my brain
before I can fall into any forest.

Behind the empty school the alderwood soothes,
quiet cascade of calm chlorophyll,
sorrowful, downward-spiralling song of hermit thrush.

Wanačis

1.
This is the mountain. I see it on the inside
of each eyelid, slanting light
through shawls of blueberry and huckleberry,
thorned thickets of baldhip rose.
Avoid the greened-over clearcut.
I say I'm picking berries.
I say I'm measuring
the disintegration of a bear scat
half way up the trail. In truth
I come because I can and it feeds us
—the mud-wallowing dog and me.
We are privileged to bypass
forgotten mining claims:
the inside of a Kokanee can
where names and dates scratched onto thin metal
were stapled to grey cedars,
their naked crowns a mark of "decadence"
made of more than decades.
Generations unabatedly unkempt.
Saved by the people in 1988.

2.
Traders called it Lone Cone, a misnomer. Undulations of dark forested land rolling southeastward on clay and nurse-log loam. Lone Cone for the lonely. Lone Cone for the solitary youth whose cry for help carried over water, brown shins scratched and bleeding from bushwhacking down wolf trails on his way south to the dock. Instead he came north to the bay. It was my honour to put him in my boat and drive him to Kakawis. On the way he taught me Wanačis, the true name of the mountain.

Canadian Patch Job

We are the country that shunted whole peoples
onto fragments of their land,
took away their children, outlawed their culture,
interned those of Japanese descent in wartime,
clear-cut the planet's safety valve
of temperate rainforests.
Now we force oil from sand,
build accident-prone pipelines,
arrest the Indigenous
with whom we hope to reconcile,
foster their children,
shoot their mothers at wellness checks,
construct dams that flood farmland
and sacred burial grounds,
breed polluting pens of diseased salmon.

I used to travel the world
smug and reassured, flaunting
my maple leaf flag-patched backpack.
I loathe hockey, love baby seals.
What can I do besides
carbon-offset every mile
sew the patch on upside-down
paint oil and tears dripping
brew reconciliAction
swap Ally for Accomplice
stay home
explain myself?

I have put off the writing of this poem long enough

The slow roast pork taco on your menu was also slow to butcher. I saw this on film: a hog hanging upside down from the ceiling still alive. There must have been a hook shoved inside or piercing fat hide. The knife as big as a man's arm, stabbed and pulled down the length of the body, pig, animal, conscious being, male or female thrashing as his or her entrails were pulled out by the human's other hand, casual. The film, silent, saved me from deafening squeals.

The scene changed and a shaved monkey sat trembling in utter defeat, beyond pitiful; scarlet slice across its head. His head; hers. Experiments for makeup or medicine, object of curiosity, investigation, the cameraman, the scientist, the assistant—not shown. Compassion, empathy, mercy—not shown. From both scenes unacknowledged life-to-life, interaction, tête-à-tête, the last relationship these animals will have with the world, unadmitted.

The monkey no longer looking to meet eyes. The sow expecting to be heard by her killer, that her pain be taken into account. And we go on to the next meal. What if humans tortured grebes? What if the hanging disembowelment was a wolf? What if we tested cosmetics on otters? What if ducklings? Bear cubs? Hawks? The mink scampering along shore doesn't know about fur farms.

Opportunity

There must be more to do besides
click on a sad-face emoji and scroll on.
How are we acceptable at eight billion,
but wild salmon disappear from rivers and seas?
While we quarantined, grey whales cavorted
in the harbour, free of speed boats,
their slicing propellers; humpbacks
dared look in at Sleilwaut. On shore,
bird droppings and blossom petals
covered parked cars while frogs crossed highways
without fear, quail-mum coaxed her chicks
anywhere she chose. In the quiet,
a grey wolf cut across the school field.
A cougar haunted Campbell Street terminus.
In England, storks returned after six centuries of absence!
They flew from Europe in a clean sky, found empty streets,
enough nest trees, a planet exhaling.
Is all we care about how soon we *return to normal*,
fill the firmament with contrails and distrails and smog?
We followed protocol to avoid spreading illness and death.
When the fires advanced and the smoke came
forcing us indoors again, two gorgeous loons
paddled up to my closed windows,
breathing our choices.

Us

In hurricane force winds before dawn
the staff room blinks out.
In the hallways fire doors are closing.
There's that brief yet too-long moment
before the backup generator kicks in.
Outside these 75-year-old walls
cracked by the last earthquake
trees have fallen, are falling in the williwaw
and those left leaning will be finished off
by scared *Homo sapiens* happy for the excuse,
forgetting new lack of living roots
could lead to flooding.
No respect for elders or future generations.
Not thinking of lungs or the needs of birds,
never dreaming of don't-see-owls or who-cares-ducks
who need hollow trees to house their young.
We work hours in fluorescent light
go home and light candles, the outdoors' quiet
broken by distant chainsawing in four directions.
Too tired to trek out onto the trails,
assess any damage. Bend from dripping
window, reach for glowing   thriving
clusters   and clusters
of sweet, dark huckleberries.

Williwaw: sudden violent squall (nautical). From MacFarlane.

Green Man

In a church, of all places,
a carved face dares—

Him, recognizable even in this
faded soft state, irrepressible,
wood shined by age,
nose chipped almost off,
there is sap yet rising—

Bend closer. He is no longer wood
but alive, laughing,
a deep voice rich as rainforest.
Grotesque challenger,
does he also grow fur, antlers?
We tremble in response,
a stirring of branches, ripples on water,
a frisson of déjà-vu (he is French, too);
familiar, those saneless eyes urging
through oak leaves,
flaming green derangement,
comic and tragic, damned paradox
of decline and arousal, the ardent gurn
eternally returning—

These walls fall away.
As our vigorous own
we might ken him and be his
as declared down through generations;
a tumble of kisses and leaves,
swirling lifetimes of matings and deaths.

HAZARD, HOME

Council Meeting: During the Break

How many trees would come down for your vacation rentals?

 On my land, lots of trees were made dangerous by the recent gale.

Instead of killing them, why not top-and-prop? Make them safe.

 Seriously?

It's done all over the world, including here. Try it some time?

 Sure, I'll get my crew to build a scaffold like we're cleaning a cathedral.

The trees here have often been called Canada's cathedrals.

 I happen to be an arborist.

Can you look at trees in a fresh light? As priorities?

 How would you like a tree to fall on you?

I'm just saying that the chainsaw is too often the first move.

 I replant; I always replant many trees.

It takes 25 years for a new tree to begin sequestering carbon. Mature trees already do that work. It may not be as easy or cheap as planting saplings.

 Eyes rolling: Are you going to say survival isn't about convenience?

Ease can be destructive.

 We need to balance the needs of people with environmental concerns.

It's perilous to separate the two. What we do to the environment, we do to ourselves.

 You're speaking in clichés.

Just tell me how many trees you want to take down, neighbour.

 Maybe a dozen.

Old growth?

 Yes.

No!

 Did you know environmentalism was started by the nazis?

There Was Wetland.

When habitats are destroyed what is lost are exquisite
ecological complexities and all the lives that make them
what they are.
—Helen Macdonald, "Tekels Park"

Where there was wetland
  you have installed parking.
    Where there was forest
      you have raised another resort.
        Who will sleep in your block-building
          when there is no more breath
          in the air; who will fatten
        your profits without clean water
      to drink? No trees for shade.
  No effort made.
What birds will sing?
You promised us.
You promised trees.
  You promised the wetland
    and its universes.
      You lied.

We Let This Happen

A letter arrives from the company. *Just a reminder!*
We'll be clearing old-growth forest and trails
in your neighbourhood starting next month, for housing.
While the mansions stay as empty as my Wins column.
Turfed out: snuffling bears, watchful owls,
chicks blinking in nests.
Goodbye quiet hush of the forest trail.
Shade, refuge, fern-cut sunlight, sanity.
An autumn of breaking and loss comes,
engines drowning out the distant surf.
Goodbye life support system, beauty.
You must make way for us,
our lights that will erase the stars.

Poem for the New Mayor

The machine chugs, spewing fumes, churning mud,
forests fall down before it,
residents attend hearings
knowing their input will be ignored
full of dread and despair, bracing for the inevitable;

machine voices present plans, exert pressure,
take their moments to further its agenda

—but you. Quietly quiet the chug.
Residents look up from their hands.
Hear words of alternative visions.
Feel their shoulders loosening, minds
blinking open in the new light.

Your gentle leadership. Others on council
chime in. Say wondrous unexpected things.
The machine has paused. Its parts
wedged, stuck on your heart.

Načiks, colonially known as Tofino

The good citizens... / cast their votes / for more of everything.
—Mary Oliver, "Extending the Airport Runway"

Four hundred generations' descendants
don't exploit this place to get rich.
They don't always have good drinking water,
or leave when someplace else catches their eye.
After thirty years I'm not a local;
my pain from watching the changes
can be nothing to theirs.
New arrivals come for surf and "spirit,"
leave their takeout cups on driftlogs,
settle in, then decide it's not good enough
without a pool, a hockey rink, a fancy gym.

To sit for Council, under fluorescent lights
reading reams of greed, I'd be faking confidence,
deciding how to approve the carving up of stolen land.
Instead I send letters, write poems, attend meetings.
The planning manager clearcuts his own property,
drills down, lowers explosives, and detonates this planet
that has sustained him and his family.
Divides thrice for maximum profit.

The mayor rides an e-bike, wants to protect forests,
opens speeches with gratitude in Nuučaańuł.
It was not under him that some of us
encased a single tree to lock out the chainsaw, not under him
a developer erased a whole woodland.

Will the word lose its meaning? Decolonize
the planning department.
Decolonize the consultants.
Decolonize land abuse, the blaster, bulldozer
driver. Decolonize the system, progress,
every cliché in our development application process.

A young man from the reserve passed out
on pavement, bottles within reach.
My pain times a thousand.
Here come the medics and police.
Let them bring red cedar, let the nurse logs
surround him, the old giants bend over him,
his people's green medicines revive him.
Return the land.
Let loose the clean water.

Spill

The oil plume spills all:
The numbers soar,
unlike the birds anymore.
Three hundred sea turtles,
shells slick under my caress.
Inside thousands of hatchlings,
their organs marinate in me.

According to the anchorman,
only one "blackened" dolphin.

Water columns stifled with the blob,
dog walkers' shoreline a killing field.
Thousands of miles away, dreams of ruined
bodies covering planes, cars and boats, coast to coast.
Wide-winged cormorants and herons draped oozing
over a prized Suzuki four-stroke outboard.

Instagram image for the nightmare files
: some nameless seabird on its back
swirling in tar, black feet in the air
because the anchorman says nothing,
for three weeks, while we wait.
Volunteers are turned away
unless willing to sign
contracts with the company.

Time to get off-grid, go home:
lower the motor, check its oil
carefully (without dripping),
start ignition. Replace guilt
with responsibility. Commit
to healing old injuries
enough to take up paddling again.
Think about rigging up a sail.

Imagine joining covert clean-up crews,
the swing of the shovel,
triumph and despair
with every capture-rescue,
a kind of pleading
with every pull on the rake.

> *I hold you in the palm of my black hand.*
> *A planet's blood belongs buried,*
> *embedded in rock*
> *soothing friction between fossils.*

Distant, estuary bound, the resident merganser
and her nine ducklings pass,
a clean line of serenity.

Nuučaańuł (Nuu-chah-nulth), Good Advice

I've been told it's time
to decolonize my mind,
that all the places I love
carry the wrong rhymes:
Lone Cone, Frank Island,
Catface, Colnett:
dubbed by and for sloop captains,
traders, missionaries, Kingdom-come,
imposing replacement.

Ts'ix-wat-sats, Chitaape,
Wałyuu: more than pretty names,
words that came up out of the land
with its peoples,
as the loon learns her song from the lake.

Try to cover a mountain in concrete?
Language keeps emerging,
the planet speaking its green poems.
In pavement's petrifaction
the newcomers postpone mortality
preserve everything in hard grey
stop death by spreading it,
lack logic.
Listen for green,
learn the names.

I've been advised not to study
French or Spanish, rather
to stand still, make roots from words,
take in the language of the place
I've made my home.

Some of What I Think I've Learned from You

for Gisele

Your language is ʔiisaac, respect,
nothing casual;
all is meaning, humour, love.
    Human words were the cosmos's links and layers.
    What we devastated with colonialism
    was cosmic expression.
Nouns were made of joined verbs,
the colour white translates
as *looks like the herring have spawned.*
Tree, Sučas, means *land holder.*
Mud slides into water courses
without forest to hold it.
Nothing is shallow,
not even dirt. Flour means

looks-like-dust, but dust
means *stuff of transformation,*
and all dust is made of ancestors.
You eat your forebears;
even flour is ancestors' dust, hence
you cherish and hold sacred your bread.

The name for crow says
give to us. You learned to speak
from the animals.
Verbed nouns
have me lost for words,
    except Love
    except Love

Notes

While there was always Indigenous presence at the peninsula's end, there was no townsite at Tofino until white settlers came here, and their first local colony was on Clayoquot or Stubbs Island. The closest Indigenous village sites remain at Opitsat, Echachist, and Hesowista (spellings vary). But a cliff at Tofino's westernmost position made a handy lookout, or guard post: Načiks. There was always a Tlaoquiaht guard at Načiks. Longhouses stood at its base.

The part of Tofino sometimes called Kwisaqs faces north, toward Opitsat. But in general all of Tofino is Načiks to the Tlaoquiaht, Ahousaht, and Hesquiaht peoples.

These nations, like others all over Turtle Island, have survived terrible injustices. Their recovery is remarkable. The retrieval of their language is a beautifully evolving process, though threatened. The gradual return of some places to their original names might seem inconvenient to non-natives. We might find them tricky to spell or a challenge to pronounce. As children in residential and day schools, the peoples of these lands were forced to learn our language. They were beaten, starved, even killed, for speaking their own. Surely settlers' descendants can make the effort to practice a few unfamiliar sounds and learn a few placenames.

Mentioned in a few of these poems, Styrofoam, in the aquatic environment, breaks down into tiny balls of EPS, or expanded polystyrene—the crumbly, chemical-laden foam used for dock floats, packaging and more. Remediating marine areas and beaches from this scale of pollution is nearly impossible, and more continues to wash ashore every day. Surfrider Canada is lobbying governments at all levels to ban this type of dock flotation. Salmon farms are a culprit. The foamfilled billets I live with were storm-salvaged. I never purchased them. I want to switch to air-filled billets and to do so is very expensive. In the meantime, I prevent leaks and even carry out guerrilla mending at other floating establishments. "It doesn't matter who you are or what you do—nobody wants billions of EPS particles all over the beach." canada.surfrider.org

"Not the Lake" was first published in *The Malahat Review*. The italicized phrase "*dilates from Earth's deep diaphragm*" was coined by Janice Lore.

"Dear Ocean" was first published in *The Goose*.

"It's a Party" was first published in *The Malahat Review*.

An earlier version of "Rain Water" was first published in *We'Moon 2023*. It was accepted for *Cascadian Zen: Bioregional Writings on Cascadia Here and Now* (Volume Two). Paul E. Nelson, Jason M. Wirth, Adelia MacWilliam and Theresa Whitehill, editors.

An earlier version of "Privilege," then named "Or Falling," was published in *Alone but Not Alone: Poetry in Isolation*. Jonathon Bigelow, editor. 2020.

"Perhaps Healed" was first published in *Quills*.

Earlier versions of "Hummadruz," "Listen From," and "Identify" were first published online with Joanna Streetly's Sound Range project at soundrange.ca/lemmens-inlet-poetry/.

An earlier version of "Pop-up Grebe" was published in *Sea & Cedar*.

"Raven" was published in *Make it True: Poetry from Cascadia*. Paul Nelson, George Stanley, Barry McKinnon and Nadine Maestas, editors. 2015.

An earlier version of "Swainson's Thrush" was first published in *The Lake*.

"Hazard, Home" was commissioned for Ekphrasis: Reversed, CVAC Verse and Vision Show 2023.

"More Perilous than a Leaning Tree" was first published in *Rising Tides: Reflections for Climate Changing Times*. Catriona Sandilands, editor. 2019.

"Town Tree Protector's To-do List" was first published in *Worth More Standing: Poets and Activists Pay Homage to Trees*. Christine Lowther, editor. 2022.

"The Child" was featured in Earthweal, a poetry forum dedicated to global witnessing of the Earth's changing climate and its effect on daily life.

An earlier version of "Nuučaańuł (Nuu-chah-nulth), Good Advice" was first published in *Make it True: Poetry from Cascadia*. The later version was first published in *Cascadian Zen: Bioregional Writings on Cascadia Here and Now* (Volume Two).

An earlier version of "Canadian Patch Job" was first published in *subTerrain*.

An earlier version of "Spill" was first published in *Make it True: Poetry from Cascadia* as "Pondering British Petroleum in Florida." It was also excerpted in my memoir, *Born Out of This*. 2014.

An earlier version of "I have put off the writing of this poem long enough" was first published in *Other Voices*.

"Opportunity" was first published in *Alone but Not Alone: Poetry in Isolation*.

Acknowledgments

A huge ʔuuščakšiƛʔick (thank you) to the ƛaʔuukwiiʔatḥ people whose lands, waters and seas have sustained me since 1992. Gisele and Levi Martin in particular as teachers of the Nuu-chah-nulth language have been generous in sharing the true names of places in their territory. Gisele was quoted in *Watershed Sentinel*, thus: "There is no 'middle of nowhere' in Indigenous lands."

I am deeply grateful to those editors who have previously published some of my work, and to the Cowichan Valley Arts Council for their commission.

Without fellow writers agreeing to read certain poems and provide feedback to them, this book would not exist. Particular thanks to Sherry Marr, Joanna Streetly, Janice Lore, Helen Mavoa, Heather Hendry, Maya Rothschild, Kathleen Shaw, Shirley Langer, Shirley Martin, David Floody, Greg Blee, Warren Rudd, Ursula Banke, Keith Ira Larkin, Tsimka Martin, Grace M. George and Terry Dorward. An additional thank you for community support from Maureen Fraser and the Tofino Arts Council.

I owe gratitude to the five authors of *Wildlife & Trees in British Columbia* (Lone Pine, 2006), many more general tree guidebooks, countless plant and fungi guides, even more bird guides, plus a few mammal and amphibian guides.

It was great fun to utilize some of the glossaries in Robert MacFarlane's *Landmarks* (Penguin, 2016). I wasn't the first, and I won't be the last. My thanks to dear friend Kate Craig for giving me that book.

I am thrilled that my sister Beth Wilks was willing to grace our front cover and other pages with her drawings in coloured pencil and metallic ink. This is our first collaboration.

I am also fathoms in debt to Vici Johnstone, Sarah Corsie and Malaika Aleba of Caitlin Press. Their dedication, meticulous attention, skills and talents have carefully and joyfully birthed this book.

About the Author

Christine Lowther resides in ƛaʔuukwiiʔatḥ (Tlaoquiaht) ha'huulthii in Nuučaańuł (Nuu-chah-nulth) territory on Vancouver Island's west coast. She is the editor of *Worth More Standing: Poets and Activists Pay Homage to Trees* and its youth companion volume, *Worth More Growing.* She is the author of three previous poetry collections. In 2014 the Pacific Rim Arts Society presented Christine with their inaugural Rainy Coast Award for Significant Accomplishment. Her memoir, *Born Out of This,* was shortlisted for the 2015 Roderick Haig-Brown Regional Prize. She won the Federation of British Columbia Writers' 2015 Nonfiction Prize and was shortlisted for the 2023 CBC Nonfiction Prize. Christine served as Tofino's Poet Laureate 2020–2022.

This book is set in Arno Pro, designed by Robert Slimbach.
The text was typeset by Vici Johnstone.
Caitlin Press, 2024.